D1237513

Love!
Poony

Grasshoppers

A Follett Beginning SCIENCE Book

SCIENCE EDUCATION CONSULTANTS

EDWARD VICTOR, Ed.D.
PROFESSOR OF SCIENCE EDUCATION
NORTHWESTERN UNIVERSITY

CURTIS MELNICK, Ed.D.
DISTRICT SUPERINTENDENT OF SCHOOLS
CHICAGO PUBLIC SCHOOLS

READING CONSULTANT

JEANNE S. BROUILLETTE
CURRICULUM COORDINATOR
EVANSTON ELEMENTARY SCHOOLS

TECHNICAL CONSULTANT

RUPERT L. WENZEL
CURATOR OF INSECTS
FIELD MUSEUM OF NATURAL HISTORY

TESTED IN THE EVANSTON PUBLIC SCHOOLS

Grasshoppers

Robert E. Pfadt
PROFESSOR OF ENTOMOLOGY
UNIVERSITY OF WYOMING

Illustrated by William R. Eastman, Jr.
and Jeanne Heitkamp

Follett Publishing Company   Chicago

Library of Congress Catalog Card Number: 66-10048

Second printing   TLA 3457

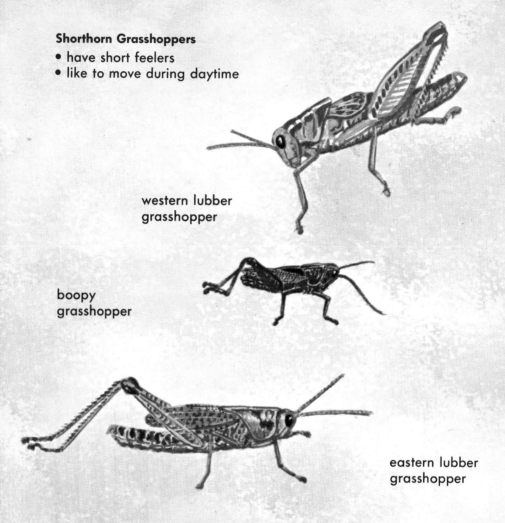

Shorthorn Grasshoppers
- have short feelers
- like to move during daytime

western lubber
grasshopper

boopy
grasshopper

eastern lubber
grasshopper

Grasshoppers are insects that live in
many places around the world. They live in
grassy fields and in farmers' crops. They even
live in the city in gardens and in weedy lots.

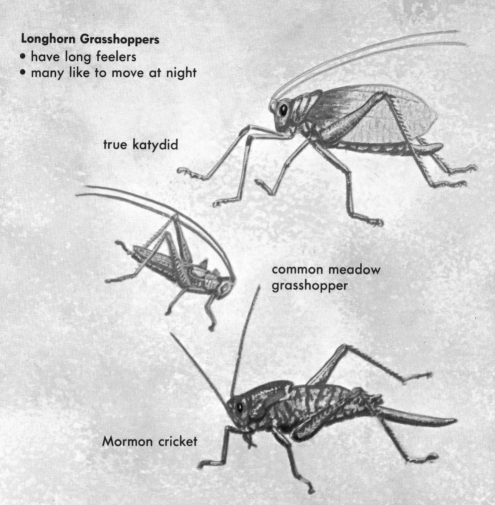

Longhorn Grasshoppers
- have long feelers
- many like to move at night

true katydid

common meadow
grasshopper

Mormon cricket

There are two families of grasshoppers.
Shorthorn grasshoppers are the kind we see
most often. This book is mostly about the
shorthorn grasshoppers. The insects in the
picture above are longhorn grasshoppers.

5

The Grasshopper's Body

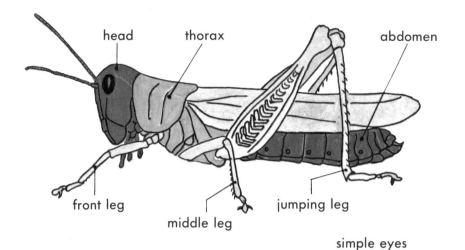

head thorax abdomen

front leg

middle leg

jumping leg

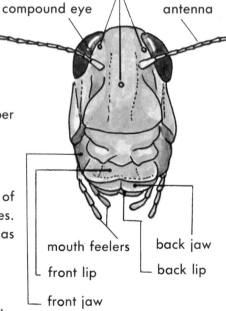

simple eyes

compound eye antenna

mouth feelers back jaw

front lip back lip

front jaw

Antennae

Each antenna helps the grasshopper to feel and smell.

Eyes

Two compound eyes are made up of thousands of small eyes, or lenses. Each of the three simple eyes has just one lens.

Mouth

The front lip helps hold food. The jaws cut the food and grind it into small pieces. The mouth feelers taste and smell food.

Grasshoppers have a hard covering on the outside of their bodies. This hard covering is the grasshopper's skin and its skeleton. Grasshoppers do not have a skeleton of bones inside their bodies, as people do. The body of the grasshopper is divided into three parts: the head, the thorax, and the abdomen.

A grasshopper sees with two large compound eyes. It also has three small simple eyes. The simple eyes can only tell changes in light. They help wake the grasshopper up.

In front of each compound eye is an antenna. The two antennae of the grasshopper act as feelers. Grasshoppers also smell with their antennae.

The mouthparts of the grasshopper are on the lower part of its head. These mouthparts are very, very strong. The picture shows the grasshopper's mouthparts.

If a boy could jump as well as a grasshopper, he could jump over a tall building.

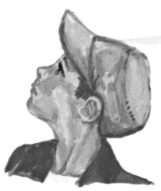

The middle part of the grasshopper's body is the thorax. On it are six legs and four wings. The two back legs of the grasshopper are much longer than the other four legs. They are even longer than the grasshopper's body. The back legs are very strong. They are used for jumping. With them, a big grasshopper can jump four feet ahead and two feet high.

8

Grasshoppers walk on all six legs. They can walk on slippery things like waxy leaves because of special pads on the bottom of their feet. Two claws at the end of each foot help the insect to climb. Grasshoppers also use their front legs to keep themselves clean.

clouded grasshopper

Grasshoppers clean or groom themselves with their legs.

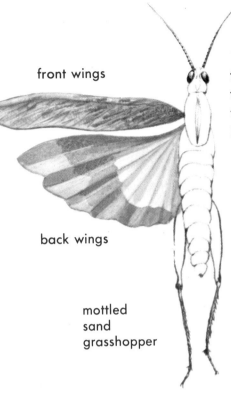

front wings

back wings

mottled
sand
grasshopper

When a grasshopper is not flying, the back wings fold up like fans. The tough front wings cover and protect them. The katydid's wings look like leaves and help it hide from enemies.

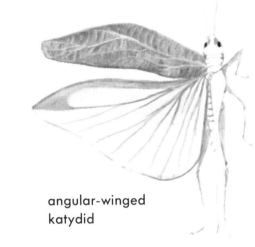

angular-winged
katydid

Grasshoppers have four wings. The two front wings are long and narrow and tough. The two back wings are wide and so thin you can see through them.

The insect uses all four wings to fly, but the two back ones do most of the work. On a calm day, grasshoppers can fly as fast as eight miles an hour. They go faster when flying with the wind.

marsh meadow
grasshopper

Grasshoppers sing by rubbing their
back legs on their front wings. The
inside of each back leg has a row of
tiny points. The front wing has a hard
ridge on it. When the points rub on
the ridge, sound is made.

Some male grasshoppers use their legs
and wings to sing. Singing is their way of
attracting female grasshoppers.

Sometimes, you can hear a loud snapping
sound when grasshoppers fly. This sound may
be another way that the insects attract each
other.

11

The rear of the grasshopper's body is the abdomen. It is made up of several rings, called segments. The insect can move and bend its abdomen easily. Its ears are on the first segment. One can tell male grasshoppers from female grasshoppers by looking at the ends of their abdomens. The picture shows how.

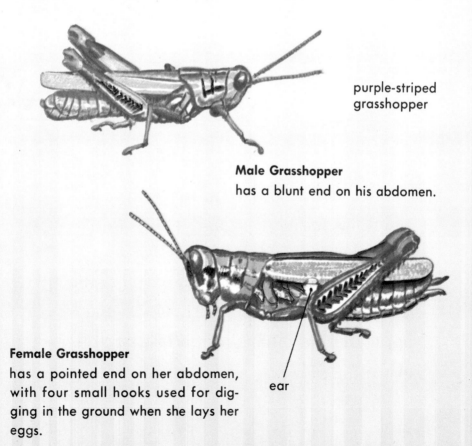

purple-striped grasshopper

Male Grasshopper
has a blunt end on his abdomen.

Female Grasshopper
has a pointed end on her abdomen, with four small hooks used for digging in the ground when she lays her eggs.

ear

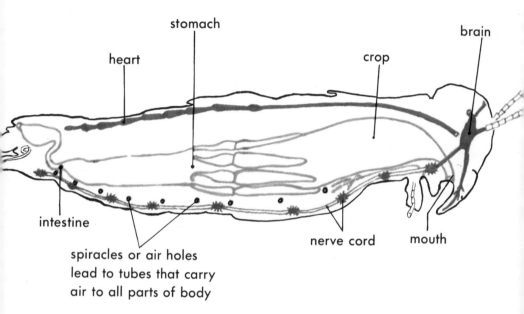

stomach

brain

heart

crop

intestine

nerve cord

mouth

spiracles or air holes
lead to tubes that carry
air to all parts of body

Grasshoppers need air to live, just as people do. But grasshoppers do not breathe in air through a nose or mouth. Instead, the insect gets air through tiny holes along each side of its body. The holes lead into tubes, which lead into smaller tubes. The tubes carry air to all parts of the grasshopper's body.

13

A grasshopper goes through
a simple metamorphosis.

1
eggs

2
nymph

A butterfly goes through
a complex metamorphosis.

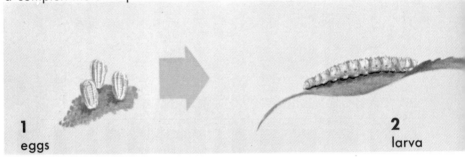

1
eggs

2
larva

Like many other insects, grasshoppers
change their form as they grow up. This change
is called metamorphosis.

14

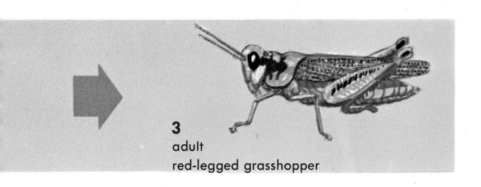

3
adult
red-legged grasshopper

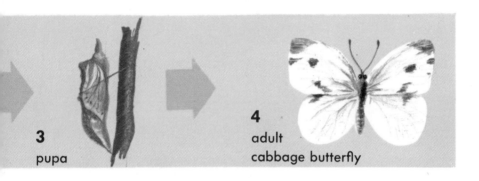

3

pupa

4
adult
cabbage butterfly

The butterfly goes through four changes during its life. We say that it has a complex metamorphosis. But the grasshopper only goes through three changes. It has a simple metamorphosis.

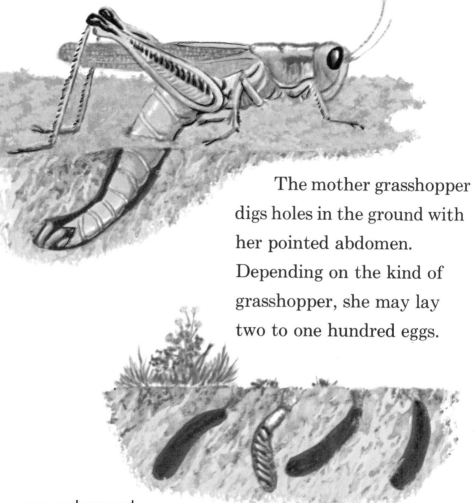

The mother grasshopper digs holes in the ground with her pointed abdomen. Depending on the kind of grasshopper, she may lay two to one hundred eggs.

eggs underground

She covers the eggs with a sticky liquid that forms a hard shell around them. This shell is called an egg pod. It protects the eggs from disease and insect enemies. Eggs laid in the summer live through the winter.

In spring, the sun warms the eggs. Soon they break open. Tiny nymph grasshoppers come out and wiggle to the top of the ground.

Newly-hatched nymphs are light-colored and soft. In a few minutes, their skins start to become darker and harder.

Nymphs look like full-grown grasshoppers, but they are smaller and do not have wings. They eat plants. The warmer the weather, the more they eat and the faster they grow.

nymphs of two-striped grasshopper

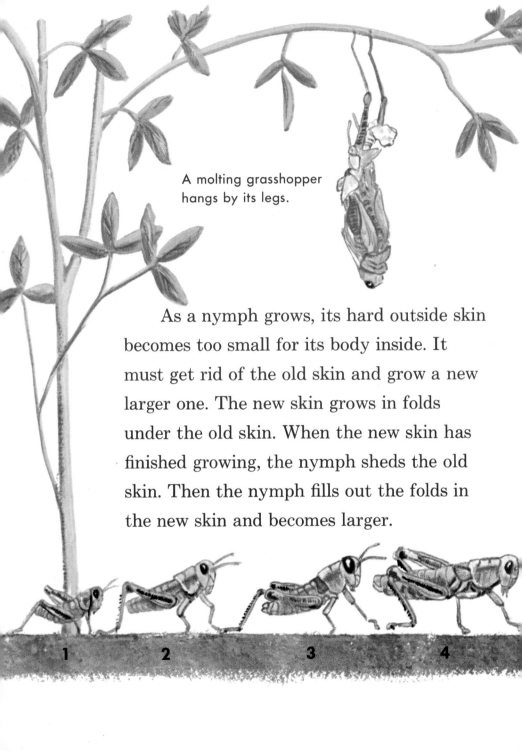

A molting grasshopper
hangs by its legs.

As a nymph grows, its hard outside skin
becomes too small for its body inside. It
must get rid of the old skin and grow a new
larger one. The new skin grows in folds
under the old skin. When the new skin has
finished growing, the nymph sheds the old
skin. Then the nymph fills out the folds in
the new skin and becomes larger.

1   2   3   4

The shedding of old skin is called molting. By molting, nymphs grow larger. They also grow wings and other adult parts.

Nymphs molt, or shed their skins, every eight to ten days. They molt five or six times before becoming adult grasshoppers with wings.

Two-striped nymphs molt five times.

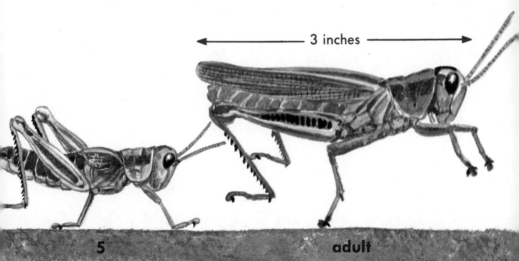

3 inches

5

adult

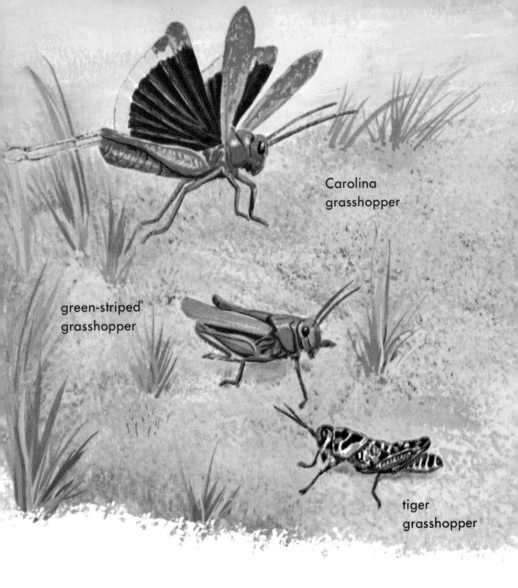

Carolina
grasshopper

green-striped
grasshopper

tiger
grasshopper

Adult grasshoppers live through the summer.
They rest in the sun. They hop and fly about.
They eat green plants.

20

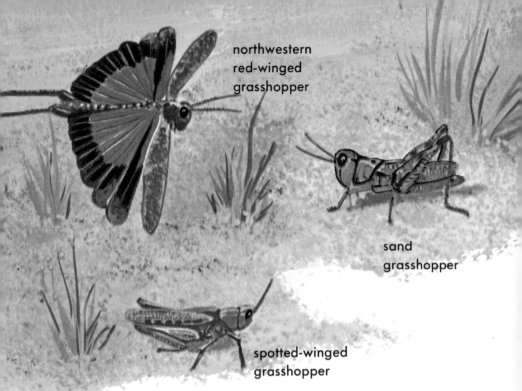

northwestern
red-winged
grasshopper

sand
grasshopper

spotted-winged
grasshopper

In summer, the male grasshoppers sing to the females. The females hear the songs and come to the males. Later, the females lay their eggs in the ground.

When cold weather comes in the fall, most of the adult grasshoppers die. Their short lives are over. But the eggs in the ground live so that new grasshoppers will hatch next spring.

Grasshoppers spit "tobacco juice" if you pick them up.

Shorthorn grasshoppers hardly ever fight with each other or with any other animal. Yet they have many enemies.

To protect themselves, grasshoppers jump or fly away. They may kick an enemy with their strong back legs. Sometimes they spit "tobacco juice," a brownish liquid, on persons who pick them up.

Birds and mice are two grasshopper enemies. They catch and eat grasshoppers. Spiders trap grasshoppers and eat them.

Some of the grasshopper's worst enemies are other insects. Robber flies catch grasshoppers and suck out the soft parts inside their bodies. Wasps feed them to their young. Some insects that live in the ground eat grasshopper eggs. Grasshoppers also die from many diseases.

Big-headed grasshopper attacked by tarantula spider.

Many kinds of grasshoppers are harmful to man. They eat plants that we need for food. Grasshoppers can do great harm if a lot of them live in one place.

Sometimes too many grasshoppers hatch in the spring. This happens when the weather is good and there are not enough grasshopper enemies in one place. The large numbers of young grasshoppers eat all the plants they can find. They eat wild plants, and they eat the farmers' plants, too. Farmers kill grasshoppers with poison.

Farmers kill harmful grasshoppers by spraying plants with poison.

24

The two-striped grasshopper eats weeds and many kinds of crops.

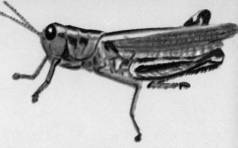

The differential grasshopper is fond of corn plants. Farmers call it the "corn hopper."

The migratory grasshopper sometimes gathers in large numbers. It can be very harmful and flies a long way. It eats many kinds of plants, and even eats clothes and curtains.

The common red-legged grasshopper often damages fields of hay.

The clear-winged grasshopper sometimes eats crops and damages mountain meadows.

Over six hundred kinds of grasshoppers live in North America. The five shown here do the most damage to crops.

Sometimes many millions of grasshoppers
gather together, or swarm. They destroy all
of the crops people need for food. In 1848,
bands of longhorn grasshoppers called Mormon
crickets began to eat the crops of settlers
around the Great Salt Lake of Utah. The
people tried to kill them, but there were
too many. It seemed that the people would
starve next winter, because the insects were
eating all their crops.

26

Suddenly a huge flock of gulls came flying to the fields. The gulls began to eat up the crickets. Soon the crickets were gone and the crops were saved. The people built a statue of a gull to show how thankful they were that the birds had come.

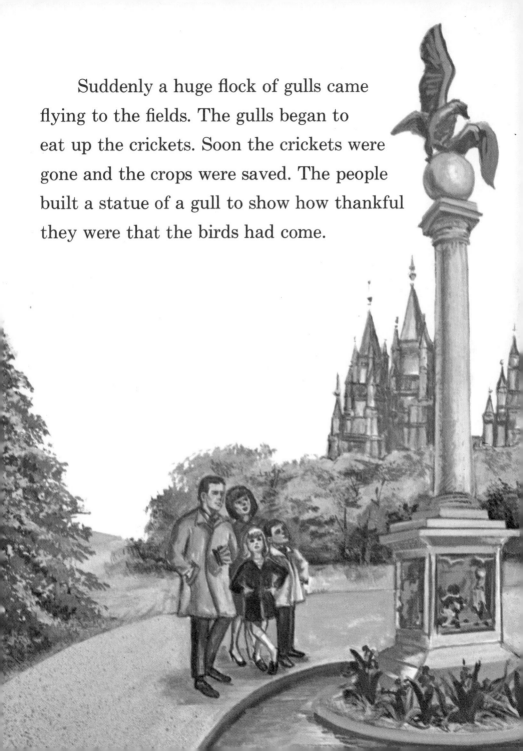

People in Iraq trying to save their crops from grasshoppers by spreading poisoned food.

Huge grasshopper swarms are not very often seen in North America today. But parts of Asia and Africa have dangerous swarms. The desert locust is a grasshopper that is a strong flier. A single swarm may have one billion insects. These grasshoppers sometimes fly across several countries, eating as they go.

28

In Bible times, the desert locust ate so many crops that people died of hunger. Even today, people in Africa, Arabia, Iraq, Pakistan and other places suffer because of locust swarms. Many countries must work together to stop the desert locust from eating crops.

The desert locust attacks crops in Africa, the Middle East, and India.

█ Area where desert locust is found

29

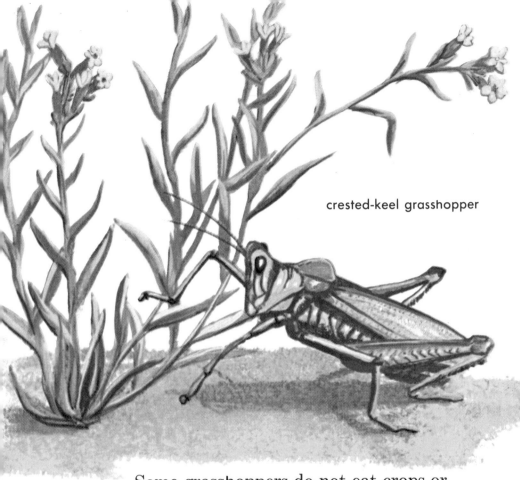
crested-keel grasshopper

Some grasshoppers do not eat crops or grass. They eat only weeds. The crested-keel grasshopper eats mostly weeds. Katydids and other longhorn grasshoppers hardly ever become pests.

Grasshoppers that do not eat crops or grass may be helpful to man.

Words Younger Children May Need Help With

(Numbers refer to page on which the word first appears.)

5	Shorthorn	11	female	22	tobacco
	meadow	12	segments		juice
	katydids	13	breathe	26	swarm
	Longhorn	14	metamorphosis		Mormon
7	skeleton	16	depending		Utah
	thorax		liquid	28	locust
	abdomen		disease	29	Iraq
	compound	17	nymph		Pakistan
	antenna		weather		
	mouthparts	19	molting		

THINGS TO DO IN SCHOOL OR AT HOME

Collect living grasshoppers. Catch a grasshopper and put it in a jar with a lid that has air holes punched in it. Watch the grasshopper eat and see how it holds and chews leaves and grass. Tap the sides of the jar and see how it jumps. Collect young nymph grasshoppers early in summer and see if you can keep them until they shed their skins. Do the insects shed the skin that covers the antennae and eyes? Is the shed skin transparent? Where did the skin split so that the grasshopper could come out?

Make a collection of dead grasshoppers. Make a net for collecting grasshoppers. A clothes hanger makes a good hoop. Fasten it to a stick with wire and tacks. Make a bag out of an old curtain or cheesecloth. After you have caught the grasshopper, pour several drops of lighter fluid (naphtha) on the insect's head. This kills it quickly and painlessly. Remove the insect from the net and place it carefully in your collecting box.

Mount and display grasshoppers. Grasshoppers should be mounted as soon as possible after you have killed them. Otherwise they will dry out and their parts will break easily. To mount a

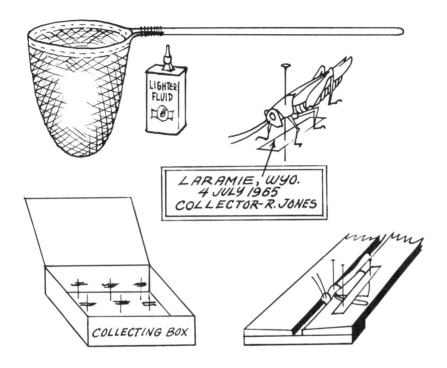

LIGHTER FLUID

LARAMIE, WYO.
4 JULY 1965
COLLECTOR-R. JONES

COLLECTING BOX

grasshopper, use either a straight pin or a mounting pin bought from a scientific supply house. Push the pin through the thorax, a little to the right of the center of the body. Straighten the legs and antennae. If you wish to display the insect with its wings out, you must first pin it to a thick cardboard with its back down. Then spread out the wings carefully so that they look something like the picture on page 10. Use empty thread spools or other small objects to hold the wings down for one day while they dry. Then remove the insect from the cardboard.

Mount it on a pin so that the pinhead is above the grasshopper's back. Put a small label on the pin just below the insect, giving its common and scientific names, the date, and the place where it was collected.